MW01697584

UNCOMMON ATHLETES:

FILLED WITH PASSION, FUELED BY PURPOSE

Tim Brown

ISBN 978-1-938254-56-7

Cross Training Publishing
www.crosstrainingpublishing.com
(308) 293-3891

All scripture quotations are taken from the NIV, ESV, The Message, and KJV. This book is manufactured in the United States of America.

Library of Congress Cataloging in Publication Data in Progress.

COMPETITOR'S CREED

I am a Christian first and last.
I am created in the likeness of God Almighty to bring Him glory.
I am a member of Team Jesus Christ. I wear the colors of the cross.

I am a Competitor now and forever. I am made to strain, to stretch and to succeed in the arena of competition. I am a Christian Competitor and as such, I face my challenger with the face of Christ.

I do not trust in myself, I do not boast in my abilities or believe in my own strength. I rely solely on the power of God. I compete for the pleasure of my Heavenly Father, the honor of Christ and the reputation of the Holy Spirit.

My attitude on and off the field is above reproach – my conduct beyond criticism. Whether I am preparing, practicing or playing: I submit to God's authority and those He has put over me. I respect my coaches, officials, teammates, and competitors out of respect for the Lord.

My body is the temple of Jesus Christ. I protect it from within and without. Nothing enters my body that does not honor the Living God. My sweat is an offering to my Master. My soreness is a sacrifice to my Savior.

I give my all – all of the time. I do not give up.
I do not give in. I do not give out. I am the Lord's warrior – a competitor by conviction and a disciple of determination.
I am confident beyond reason because my confidence lives in Christ.
The results of my efforts must result in His glory.

Let the competition begin. Let the glory be God's.

FELLOWSHIP OF CHRISTIAN ATHLETES

Sign the Creed @ www. fca.org

Contents

CONTACTING THE AUTHOR

Tim Brown is an author, educator, coach, and motivational speaker who has inspired youth and adults in the Central Ohio area for more than a decade. He is an ordained minister and serves as a Camp Ministry Director for the Fellowship of Christian Athletes (FCA).

Tim has used his unique combination of skills and experiences to create the essence of his new book release, **Uncommon Athletes**, a powerful and insightful book that is the second in the Uncommon Life series. **Uncommon Athletes** was written to challenge athletes to develop an uncommon identity and find the path that leads to greatness.

Coach Brown is a chaplain for several area high school sports teams and speaks at FCA Huddles, Churches, and Youth Conferences. He has served as a chapel speaker for Ohio Dominican and Ohio State Universities, Otterbein College, University of Illinois and the University of Akron football teams. Tim has led workshops at Akron, Bowling Green, Kent State, Ohio and Savannah State Universities. He has been a school assembly speaker, leads Boys Won't Be Boys Uncommon Life Book Clubs at schools and has spoken at the "Men's Rally in the Valley" in Youngstown, Ohio.

Tim is a native of East Cleveland, Ohio. He received his B.A. from Ohio University and began his professional career in Columbus, Ohio, where he resides with his wife and children.

Contact Information for Tim Brown:
tbrown@fca.org or 614.496.1794
Follow Coach Tim Brown on Facebook and Twitter @brown_coach

Preface

How do I use this book? This book is designed to help you and your teammates build your character. It is important that you take enough time during your meetings (approximately 29-40 minutes) to go through each section of the study. Each week you will have the opportunity to talk about how you were able to build your character since the previous Team Bible Study. After this time of catching up, you will do a warm up to introduce this week's character trait. This will include a team building exercise. If you have time you could do this as a group. You might even suggest to your coach your whole team could do this outside of the Team Bible Study. After this warm up you will have the opportunity to look into the ultimate source of character building—the Bible—and discover how it might guide you as you build your character.

What is a Team Bible Study? A Team Bible Study is a group of athletes from a team desiring to discuss real life and build their character through God's principles.

How big should a Team Bible Study be? This is hard to say, but generally people feel most comfortable talking and learning in a group of 10 or fewer. The bottom line is that those on your team who want to be involved should have the chance, if it is only 3 or even if it is more than 20.

When should we meet? Team Bible Study groups typically meet during the team's season. The best time to do it is before or after practice, so you are not adding another time commitment to your already busy life.

How can I get the most out of this? You will get out of this exactly what you put into it. How honest you are with yourself and the others in the group will determine how much you will get out of this. It might be a stretch for some of you to risk being vulnerable for the first time.

Who can lead a Team Bible Study? Team Bible Studies are best led by someone connected with your team! It could be a player, coach, assistant coach, chaplain, etc. It is not difficult to lead a Team Bible Study. You don't have to be an expert in any particular area.

What is the Gospel? Christians often say that Jesus died for our sins. But what does that mean? Why did He die? What has He accomplished by His death on the cross? What effect does His death on a cross have on us? With this book, we have selected key themes that focus on the Gospel with each character trait. However, to be clear, here are the Gospel facts you should repeatedly review with your students.

Gospel Facts: That the one and only one God, who is holy, made us in His image to know Him. However, we have sinned and cut ourselves off from Him. Because of God's love for us, God became a man in Jesus, lived a perfect life, and died on the cross. He fulfilled the law Himself by taking on the punishment we deserved for the sins of all those who ever turn to and trust Him. He rose again from the dead, showing that God accepted Christ's sacrifice and that God's wrath against us had been exhausted. Now, God calls us to repent of our sins and trust in Christ, we are born again into a new life, an eternal life with God.

Team Bible Study Commitments

- Priority--As long as you are a part of the Team Bible Study, you must make the meetings a priority.
- Participation--Everyone participates, no one dominates.
- Respect--Everyone is given the right to his own opinion, and all questions are encouraged and respected.
- Confidentiality--Anything that is said in the group stays in the group and is never repeated outside of the meeting.
- Empty Chair--The group remains open to new teammates.
- Support--Permission is given to call upon each other in times of need--even in the middle of the night.
- Giving Advice--Unsolicited advice is not allowed.
- Multiplication--We agree to do everything in our power to pray that others on your team would be interested in developing their character through God's principles.

STUDY 1

PREPARATION

UNCOMMON PREPARATION

Remind the people...to be ready to do whatever is good. Titus 3:1

Jerry Rice is an uncommon athlete. One of the greatest wide receivers ever to play professional football, Rice had over 200 touchdowns, 1,500 receptions, and 22,000 receiving yards during his twenty-year career in the NFL. Because of his performances, he was named MVP of Super Bowl XXIII and, in 2010, was inducted into the NFL Hall of Fame.

Without a doubt, Rice is a talented football player. But he did not become the most effective wide receiver in NFL history merely because of his talent. Many other talented players never achieve the level of skill that Rice maintained for two decades. Instead, Jerry Rice will tell you his success was directly related to the thousands of hours he spent preparing for every game, every season.

He said, "I don't think I'm such a natural, I think what I'm doing is very hard work. I work hard to keep in shape, I work hard on the practice field, I work hard in a game. It isn't easy."

Think about it: The fortuity of life comes more often as preparation becomes a practice.

1. Have you ever been called to go into a game to replace a teammate? Did you feel prepared? Why or why not?

2. Share about a time when you saw an athlete or team show up unprepared? What happened?

Uncommon athletes practice with a purpose. They come to practice every day, prepared to work hard physically and mentally. They prepare for every game diligently, keeping themselves in peak condition because once the competition starts, they would rather have it and not need it, than need it and not be prepared for it.

Jerry Rice's hard work took place on "the hill" in San Francisco. Every day, Rice ran 2.5 miles uphill without stopping, even during the off-season. "A lot of professional players would wait until training camp to work themselves into shape. I would take two weeks off during the off-season, then go right back into my regimen." Few other athletes prepared as Jerry Rice did. But because he worked beforehand, he achieved amazing things.

Uncommon athletes also practice hard at every level because they understand that today's preparation leads to tomorrow's victories. They develop the habit of uncommon preparation, from peewee league to varsity, because talent is never enough to ensure final victory. Uncommon athletes know they must always show up prepared.

Uncommon athletes also practice to become leaders. As Jerry Rice powerfully illustrates, uncommon preparation paves the way for two powerful results:

Success. Success and glory may come to us, but they are more likely to come when we work hard to achieve them. Uncommon preparation allows you to perform at your peak when the game begins, giving you a greater chance to win the game. It gives you the power and instinct to be great when it matters most. Uncommon preparation, being "all in" in practice, in games, and in life, is what will bring success later.

Influence. Uncommon preparation produces a superior athlete who is effective during competition and who quickly becomes a leader on the team. The uncommon athlete is always ready, and the entire team knows it. The coach trusts him. Her teammates depend on her. The uncommon athlete becomes irreplaceable, the one everyone looks to when the game is on the line. That is the power of preparation.

WORKOUT

1. Describe someone you think displays a commitment to uncommon preparation?

2. What do you do that is uncommon to prepare for the game?

3. Why is it hard for most athletes to live out uncommon preparation?

WRAPUP

The moment preparation turns into action can be intimidating. Tension builds as the entire team waits in position for the whistle that will start the game. Everyone is ready to see just how prepared they really are. In the same way, in Joshua, chapter 1, God's people, Israel, stood at the entrance to the land God had promised to give them. After wandering in the desert for forty years because of their disobedience, this was their big moment. They waited only for God's signal to go.

But before God sent the people in, He challenged Joshua, their new leader, to put his own preparation into action. "Moses my servant is dead. Now then, you and all these people, get ready to cross the Jordan River into the land I am about to give to them" (Joshua 1:2).

1. Do you think it was easy for Joshua to step into Moses' place and lead the people forward?

This was Joshua's championship game. It was a big risk to try to conquer their enemies, but he was prepared. He had spent forty years as Moses' second-in-command. He had led God's people into battle. He had watched Moses make decisions, trust God, and lead the people through every possible problem. And now it was up to him.

WRAPUP

2. Forty years is a long time to prepare. Do you think Joshua always understood how what he experienced in those forty years was preparing him for future success?

3. Does what you do in practice always make sense (running laps, doing drills, stretches)? What can you do to stay focused even when your preparation doesn't seem to be useful?

God gave Joshua one final order. "Be strong and courageous. Do not be afraid; do not be discouraged, for the LORD your God will be with you wherever you go" (Joshua 1:9). God was saying, "You are ready, Joshua. Don't be afraid. All your preparation is going to pay off because I will be with you to lead you, just as I led Moses."

4. God told Joshua to have courage and do what he had prepared to do. Who reminds you to stay focused on your preparation?

Like Joshua, we have to be prepared when our big moment comes. In sports and in life, we have to work hard ahead of time so we are always ready to handle whatever challenges we face. Whether it's a big game or a final exam, our preparation will determine whether we succeed or fail. It is not always easy. But it is uncommon.

5. Read Titus 3:1. Why do we have to be reminded to be ready to do what is good?

BE UNCOMMON

Uncommon athletes understand that struggle is the breeding ground for success. The Apostle Paul said, "We know that suffering produces perseverance; perseverance, character; and character, hope" (Rom. 5:3-4). Paul did not avoid hard things because he knew they prepared him for future glory. In the same way, uncommon athletes commit themselves to getting to practice, being on time, and pushing themselves to get better. In sports and in life, you will find yourself ready when your big moment comes when you've put yourself through a thousand small moments of preparation first.

STUDY 2

ATTITUDE

UNCOMMON ATTITUDE

God isn't late with his promise . . . He's giving everyone space and time to change. 2 Peter 3:8-9 (The Message)

In 2014, Lauren Hill was a high school senior planning to play basketball for Mount St. Joseph University—until a doctor's visit revealed she had a brain tumor. An inoperable brain tumor.

Tests revealed that she had a rare form of cancer, and she was given less than two years to live. But instead of quitting, Lauren adjusted. She continued to play ball, fighting through the negative effects of her tumor, and she started a nonprofit organization to raise money and awareness for the cancer she was fighting. And that fall, she started school at Mount St. Joseph, playing in their season opener (which the NCAA allowed them to play early so she could participate) in November.

Lauren had to stop playing in December of 2014, and she passed away in April 2015. But Lauren was an uncommon athlete. Her attitude was unbeatable, and she did not shrink from difficulty. Instead, she accepted the change, adjusted her plan, and kept on living (and playing) an uncommon life.

Think about it: If you're adaptable and nimble, that's great, because that's exactly what life requires you to be.

1. Are you good at making adjustments or do you prefer to have a plan and stick to it?

2. Why is it so important in sports to develop an attitude that can adjust?

3. Which of your teammates do you think does a good job adjusting? Why?

Uncommon athletes know that things don't always happen according to plan. They know that during competition, a play may be changed. A call may go against the team. Something totally unexpected may happen. In those moments, they adjust. Still, it is rare for any athlete, even an uncommon one, to have a Plan B already in place when changes come. It can be hard to accept the need for a change and even uncommon athletes will need time to come up with a new plan that will actually work.

That's what happened to Braxton Miller. The former quarterback of The Ohio State Buckeyes missed the 2014 season with a shoulder injury. When he returned, he was no longer able to throw long, so Miller made secret plans to change positions to wide receiver. He knew it was a risky move, but he was committed to making it work. He had to learn new skills and work hard, with no promises that he would still make it to the NFL. But Miller had an attitude of adjustment. He pushed into the unknown, and he succeeded when, in April 2016, he was drafted by the Houston Texans.

Braxton Miller's willingness to adjust makes him an uncommon athlete, but any athlete can develop this attitude. Developing an attitude of adjustment requires perspective and persistence. Having perspective means seeing today's plan, without losing sight of the long-term goals. Miller still wanted to play in the NFL, so he changed his everyday plans to make that happen. In the same way, uncommon athletes know the plan for this game and this season, but they also see the big picture. Yes, they want to win the game, but they also want to be a winner at life. They want to make the big plays, but not at the risk of injury to themselves or others. They believe in themselves, but they know that cockiness is not the same thing as confidence. They have perspective.

Uncommon adjustment is also about having persistence. Making adjustments, during a game and in life, is hard. It takes time, effort, and many mistakes. Braxton Miller practiced late at night, learning new routes, new stances, a new way of seeing the field. Many times it would have been easier to give up. But he kept going. An uncommon athlete always keeps going. They have persistence; they never, ever give up.

WORKOUT

1. Have you ever had to make a major adjustment in your sport? Was it hard to do?

2. How does having a good perspective help you deal with change?

3. Is it hard to be persistent? How can you motivate yourself to keep going in moments when you feel like giving up?

WRAPUP

In life, as in sports, we will have to make adjustments. From Abraham to Paul, from Jonah to Mary, God has often called His people to change course, to follow Him down a new and different path. His direction doesn't always make sense at the time. Sometimes, it downright hurts. But uncommon living means that even when it's hard, we choose to adjust when we prefer to stay right where we are.

Daniel knew all about adjustments. He was a young man in Jerusalem, most likely a nobleman's son, when King Nebuchadnezzar came from Babylon and conquered Israel. With the fall of Jerusalem, suddenly everything about his life was different. His family and home were destroyed. He was taken captive to Babylon and placed in the King's service. His hope, his future, his plans—all gone.

But as we watch Daniel's story unfold in the book of Daniel, chapter 1, he demonstrates for us three key habits of an uncommon attitude.

First, he was not controlled by his feelings. Our emotions are important. They are powerful indicators that help us deal with life. But how we feel does not have to affect our ability to roll with the punches. Daniel knew this, and "he resolved" to deal with his new situation so that, no matter what happened to him, God would be pleased with him (Dan. 1:8). No matter how

WRAPUP

Daniel felt, no matter how scared or angry or upset he was, he made up his mind to adjust his plans and accept the new path God had placed him on. And because of his decision to live uncommonly, God honored him and gave him favor with his captors.

Second, Daniel didn't compare himself. No matter what the other captives did or how they reacted, Daniel did not let them define his choices. He focused on doing his thing and doing it to the best of his ability, even though he was far from home and facing a life much different than what he'd had planned.

Third, Daniel trusted God. He could have yelled at God and blamed Him for all the bad things that had happened to him. He could have thrown a fit and made life miserable for his captors. But instead, he trusted God and remained faithful. When tough changes come our way, we must choose to trust that God is good. Then we can commit our future into His capable hands and keep going strong. Just like Daniel.

1. God often asks us to change a behavior, an attitude, or a way of thinking. Is it easy or hard to make the changes God requires?

2. Why doesn't comparing ourselves to others help us make adjustments, in sports or in life?

3. We cannot control our circumstances, but we can control our attitude. Do you agree or disagree? How can you apply this principle when changes come into your life?

BE UNCOMMON

Adjustments are a necessary part of life. But if we know where we want to go, in sports and in life, we can deal with detours as they come. Ask yourself what you want your life to look like in 5 years, 10 years, 15 years. Do you want to go to college? Play varsity? Own a business? Have a good reputation? Write down your goal. Then write down the steps you need to take to reach that goal. Next, start putting those steps into practice. We cannot escape tough times in life. But with an uncommon attitude of adjustment we can ultimately, succeed.

STUDY 3

SACRIFICE

UNCOMMON SACRIFICE

Therefore, I urge you, brothers and sisters, in view of God's mercy, to offer your bodies as a living sacrifice, holy and pleasing to God—this is your true and proper worship. Romans 12:1

In 2015, Carli Lloyd scored three goals against Japan in the first 16 minutes of the World Cup Finals, leading the women's team to their third World Cup Championship and making her the first woman ever to score a hat trick in the World Cup Finals.

But Lloyd's success was not an accident. In fact, she began training for that Finals win in 2003. For Carli Lloyd, sacrifice is the name of the game. For the last decade, she has trained twice a day, nearly every day. She pushes herself mentally and physically to strengthen her game. And after her World Cup win she declared, "I've dedicated my whole life to this. Everything comes second."

Carli Lloyd demonstrates the uncommon sacrifice necessary to become a great athlete. The hours of practice, the physical challenges, the mental effort are all worth it because they help her achieve great things. That is the mindset that every uncommon athlete must develop. Sacrifice always comes before success. No one can become great without giving up lesser things first.

Think about it: Surrendering yourself for a greater good isn't giving up who you are; it's the master key to discovering who you can be.

1. We sacrifice for whatever we think is truly important. Do you agree or not? How do you personally sacrifice for your sport?

Chris Spielman knows what it is to sacrifice. His hard work and skill made him a formidable lineman at every level of football. He was the first high school athlete to be featured on the front of a Wheaties box. As a college athlete, he won the Lombardi Award. And between 1988 and 1997, he played for the Detroit Lions and the Buffalo Bills, appearing in multiple Pro Bowls and setting records with both organizations.

But Spielman was uncommon off the gridiron, too, when his wife was diagnosed with breast cancer in 1998. He shaved his head when chemotherapy made her hair fall out, and he publicly made Stefanie his highest priority. He was so committed to helping his wife fight her disease that he chose to miss the 1998 season to be with her. Even when the combination of her cancer and a neck injury forced his retirement in 1999, the Spielmans continued to fight against breast cancer, using their fame to raise money and awareness for breast cancer research.

In those years, like never before, Chris Spielman displayed uncommon sacrifice. He had to learn to put down his ego and his obsession with football in order to care for and support his wife. But it wasn't an easy shift for Spielman to make. When her cancer came back for the fourth time, he finally learned to ask for help.

Uncommon sacrifice takes time and effort; it isn't easy. It means making hard trades, giving up your time or energy or something that you want very much in order to gain something even greater. In his battle, Chris Spielman gained faith, patience and a lifelong mission to fight against cancer with the same passion he displayed on the football field.

In November 2009, Stefanie Spielman died after her cancer returned for the fifth time. But in the years since her death, Chris Spielman has continued to sacrifice for his family. He now balances his broadcasting schedule and the needs of his children. He continues to raise money and awareness for breast cancer, and his sacrifices have earned him an enduring place not just in football history, but in the lives of many who have been touched by his uncommon sacrifice.

WORKOUT

1. Why is sacrifice necessary for success during competition?

2. Share about someone you know who, like Chris Spielman, has sacrificed greatly, on or off the field.

3. What kind of sacrifices can a team make together that will help them grow as players and as people?

WRAPUP

No success will ever come without sacrifice. It's true in practice and in the weight room. It's true on the field and during the game. And it's true in life.

Living uncommonly means we choose to sacrifice at school, at a job, and in our homes, so that we can become the best version of ourselves we can be.

But even more importantly, sacrifice is important for spiritual success. Our greatest example of sacrifice is, of course, Jesus Christ, who "loved us and gave himself up for us as a fragrant offering and sacrifice to God" (Eph. 5:2). He gave up his throne in heaven to be born a human, live among us, and be crucified so that, through his resurrection, we could be redeemed. We are alive spiritually because of His sacrifice.

And God expects us to sacrifice, too. To give up what we want (our own comfort or success, for example) to gain what He wants for us. That's why, in Romans 12:1, Paul commands us to "offer your bodies as a living sacrifice, holy and pleasing to God." Our greatest act of worship will always be to offer ourselves to God first, living a life of sacrifice in response to all He has done for us.

But sacrifice in God's economy is more than giving money to

WRAPUP

charity or showing up for church on Sunday when you'd rather sleep in. To achieve great things spiritually, we have to go deeper than that.

Read the following verses. What sacrifice is named in each passage? What is God asking us to give up? What benefit will we gain if we choose sacrifice?

1. Hebrews 13:16 – And do not forget to do good and to share with others, for with such sacrifices God is pleased.

2. Hebrews 13:15 – Through Jesus, therefore, let us continually offer to God a sacrifice of praise—the fruit of lips that openly profess his name.

3. Psalm 51:17 – My sacrifice, O God, is a broken spirit; a broken and contrite heart you, God, will not despise.

4. 2 Samuel 24:24-25 – But the king replied to Araunah, "No, I insist on paying you for it. I will not sacrifice to the Lord my God burnt offerings that cost me nothing." So David bought the threshing floor and the oxen and paid fifty shekels of silver for them. David built an altar to the Lord there and sacrificed burnt offerings and fellowship offerings. Then the Lord answered his prayer in behalf of the land, and the plague on Israel was stopped.

God calls us to give up the lesser things in our lives to achieve the greater things. This is what it means to choose uncommon sacrifice.

BE UNCOMMON

Whatever your goal is—beating that video game, getting an A, making a difference in your school or neighborhood—it can only be achieved with uncommon sacrifice. It means giving up lesser things so you have time and energy to do better things. Not watching TV so you can do your homework. Saving your cash instead of spending it. Staying home on Saturday night so you don't get sucked into unwise or illegal things. Those are the uncommon sacrifices that will build toward great success, in sports and in life.

SELFLESSNESS

UNCOMMON SELFLESSNESS

Do nothing out of selfish ambition or vain conceit. Rather, in humility value others above yourselves, not looking to your own interests, but each of you to the interests of others. Philippians 2:3-4

In many ways, Red Auerbach revolutionized the game of basketball. He drafted the first African-American player in 1950 and, over the years, crafted a Boston Celtics organization that dominated the basketball court. As a coach, he almost single-handedly changed how basketball was played. He is often credited with creating the position of the "sixth man."

The sixth man doesn't start most games. He is not the player people pay to see. Instead, the sixth man comes off the bench during the game to play wherever he is most needed. This player often covers more than one position, he is a master of offense and defense, and most importantly, he displays uncommon selflessness. While many of today's players demand the spotlight, the sixth man puts the needs of the team above himself. He wants the team to succeed more than he wants to be a star. And to honor the special selflessness that the sixth man displays, the NBA created the Sixth Man of the Year award to recognize these players who support their team from the bench with excellence.

Think about it: When you become a selfless team, you'll soon be a winning team.

1. Why is selflessness such an uncommon quality among athletes?

2. Can you think of an athlete who demonstrates this kind of unselfishness?

In 2012, Steph Curry signed a four-year, $44 million rookie contract extension with the Golden State Warriors. In 2015, Curry led the team to an NBA Championship and was named League MVP, which means he is a Most Valuable Player whose salary is only fifth-highest on his team. When Curry signed his contract extension, his future was uncertain. Now that his dominance on the court has been established, his salary is well below what he is worth. But it is precisely in situations like these that uncommon selflessness shines.

First, selflessness requires a firm foundation. No matter what happens, selfless athletes say, "I know who I am, I know what my goal is, and I'm willing to give up my preferences to achieve that goal." They put the game and the team above themselves.

Curry is a great example of this. While he admits that it's hard not to focus on his salary, he refuses to let it distract him. "I had to make a conscious decision and remind myself over and over [to let it go]...You can't look back, because it'll bring negativity. It'll cause dissension in the team if you allow it to." Curry is not willing to risk the team and its goals over his pay. That is uncommon selflessness.

But secondly, selflessness focuses on the positive. It's not enough to give up our rights for others, to simply not retaliate when we don't get our way. We also have to do whatever we do with the right attitude. We can gripe; we can complain. We can tell everyone who will listen how bad we've got it. But that is not uncommon. Instead, choosing selflessness means giving up my way and doing it cheerfully, even gratefully. Curry says, "I've tried to just be appreciative of what I have. I'm taken care of, and I'm thankful that I can be on the court able to play at a high level. I'm thankful it's not the other way around, that I didn't become an overpaid player. That's a different conversation."

Even though his pay does not match his true value as a player, Steph Curry demonstrates uncommon selflessness. We can too. We need to keep our perspective on our goals instead of on ourselves and choose to be grateful even when life, or the game, or the referee's call, doesn't go our way.

WORKOUT

1. How often do you see this kind of selflessness in your sport? Is it common? If not, what is a more common way for athletes to behave?

2. List three ways a team might behave selfishly. Now list three ways your team can display uncommon selflessness.

3. Why is gratitude so important? How can you practice being more thankful?

WRAPUP

Surprisingly, the key to uncommon selflessness is comparison. But only the right kind. In the world of sports, comparisons are everywhere. Who is better: Steph Curry or LeBron James? Does the SEC really outrank the Big 10? Who is the best golfer (or boxer or surfer or gymnast) in the world? No matter the sport, people analyze every move and every stat, comparing athletes and teams to determine who is, or is not, the very best. In sports and in life, we can expect comparisons. But not every comparison is a good idea.

When we compare ourselves to others: our friends, our teammates, our opponents, we will always lose. Other people are moving targets. They are basically just like us and cannot give us a sense of stability. Comparing ourselves to other people always results in self-doubt (because they seem better) or an ego trip (because we seem better). And neither of those responses leads to uncommon selflessness.

1. Do you compare yourself to other people? What happens when you do?

Instead, an uncommon athlete cultivates humility. That's what Paul tells us in the book of Philippians where he commands the church to "do nothing out of selfish ambition or vain conceit. Rather, in humility value others above yourselves, not looking to your own interests, but each of you to the interests of others" (Phil. 2:3-4).

Do nothing, Paul says, that is about making yourself look or sound better. Instead, treat other people like they are more valuable than you are. Don't worry so much about protecting yourself, but instead, look for ways you can protect other people. Do this, Paul says, because you have "the same mindset as Christ Jesus" (v.5).

2. It's easy to want to put ourselves first. But what would it look like for you, or your team, to make protecting each other a priority?

Uncommon athletes know that comparing themselves to others will always end in defeat. Instead, the path to uncommon selflessness means comparing themselves to Jesus, the ultimate example of humility. Jesus refused to lord His power over us; He came as a baby. He deserved heaven, but He gave it up to save us. He is God, but He died for our sins. And when we compare ourselves to Him, we no longer have the option of demanding our own way. Like Him, we lay down our lives, our preferences, our selfishness so that, like Him, we can display uncommon selflessness.

3. Read Philippians 2:1-11. What would it look like to apply them on your team or in competition?

Uncommon selflessness comes when we put others first. Whether we are on the field, in practice, in school, or at home, we can choose the "mindset of Christ Jesus" and become truly uncommon.

BE UNCOMMON

Choosing selflessness can be difficult. Being humble might mean somebody could take advantage of you. It might mean giving up a position or a play that you desperately wanted to have. But living selflessly always leads to a life of greater significance. Selfless athletes play for their teammates. They give great effort and play with great spirit so that they don't let down their team. And this commitment to making others better, while sometimes costly in the short-run, makes for richer relationships, stronger teams, and greater victories in the long run. Uncommon athletes are selfless.

STUDY 5

INTEGRITY

UNCOMMON INTEGRITY

Whoever walks in integrity walks securely, but whoever takes crooked paths will be found out. Proverbs 10:9

In 2010, Jeremy Affeldt, a relief pitcher for the San Francisco Giants, signed a $10 million contract extension. But an error in the contract meant the Giants organization was paying him an extra $500,000, on top of his actual salary. When he realized the error, Affeldt got a number of opinions about what he should do. Legally, everyone said, the money was his to keep.

But Affeldt gave it back. After discussing the unintended bonus with his agent and with the Giants, Affeldt had the contract rewritten to fix the error. He told them, "I can't take that money. I won't sleep well at night knowing I took that money because every time I open my paycheck I'll know it's not right."

Jeremy Affeldt is a great example of uncommon integrity. When he realized the contract was incorrect, he revealed it instead of hiding it. When he could have kept the money, he gave it back. In other words, even though it cost him, he did the right thing. This is the mark of an uncommon athlete.

Think about it: Integrity is a trait we're all capable of having—and should have—but manifesting it daily is the test we're graded on . . . forever.

1. If you were Jeremy Affeldt, would you have given the money back?

2. How do you define integrity? What does that word mean to you? Why is integrity so important?

Uncommon integrity is a guardrail for your life. Like wearing a seatbelt in a car or wearing safety gear during competition, maintaining uncommon integrity keeps you safe. It keeps your life from collapsing around you. Some athletes take this truth seriously, and they choose their actions and words carefully. But every day, we see the stories of athletes who are living without integrity plastered all over sports blogs and ESPN. As Proverbs 10:9 says, "Whoever walks in integrity walks securely, but whoever takes crooked paths will be found out."

Lance Armstrong learned this lesson the hard way. For over a decade, Armstrong denied taking performance enhancing drugs. When he finally admitted to doping, he lost his integrity, his reputation, and all of his Tour de France titles. Even the foundation he created cut its ties with him. As Armstrong found out, integrity is not about what you say, but what you do...or don't do.

But it is possible to find examples of uncommon integrity, too. In the book of Genesis, Joseph was sold into slavery by his brothers and bought by Potiphar, an Egyptian official. Everything Joseph touched went well because God was with him, and Potiphar put everything he owned under Joseph's control. Everything except his wife.

Unfortunately, Joseph was the one thing Potiphar's wife wanted. She invited him to sleep with her again and again, but Joseph refused. He had lots of good reasons why he could have done it. He'd been the favored son; now he was a slave. Potiphar didn't pay attention to what went on in his household because Joseph handled things so well; Joseph probably could have gotten away with it without Potiphar ever knowing about it.

But Joseph would have known. And Joseph knew that God was watching how he lived, too. So he kept his integrity and refused her advances. Of course, eventually, she falsely accused him of seducing her, and Joseph was thrown in prison. But because he acted with integrity, God was pleased with Joseph. And He continued to bless Joesph, even in prison.

WORKOUT

1. Have you ever been in a tempting situation like Joseph or Jeremy Affeldt? How did you handle it?

2. Read Proverbs 10:9 again. What are some "crooked paths" you know you should avoid?

3. Look up Genesis 39:8-10. What does it mean to not sin against God?

WRAPUP

Integrity means following the rules and playing fair. But uncommon integrity goes even farther. Uncommon integrity means doing the right thing, even when no one is watching and even if it costs you the game. Or the record.

Senior Nate Hassis was just 29 yards shy of the conference passing yard record, with 30 seconds left in his final game, when his coach called a time-out to talk with their opponents. When play resumed, it was clear the coaches had "arranged" for Hassis to break the record. His pass went to a wide-open receiver who ran 37 yards, giving him the record. Except it didn't.

Hassis refused to accept a record that wasn't won fairly. He wrote a letter and asked that the pass be removed from his stats. That is uncommon integrity.

And even though doing the right thing sometimes costs you, it also gives you great influence. With your coach, on your team, and in life. When you have uncommon integrity, people will trust that you say what you mean and do what you say. And because they trust you, they'll follow you.

This kind of influence cannot be swayed by peer pressure. When others lie, cut corners in practice, or disobey the coach, the uncommon athlete stands his or her ground. He will do the right thing, and his integrity will inspire his teammates to join him. In fact, his teammates will

WRAPUP

know that he won't stand for a poor work ethic. Athletic integrity means giving your all. It says, "Work hard or go home." An uncommon athlete is always willing to go the extra mile in practice and in the game, and he expects his teammates to do the same.

Excuses. An uncommon athlete refuses to give excuses, and she won't hear them from her teammates. Integrity means finding a way to get the job done with no excuses.

Disrespect. Uncommon athletes won't allow another player to misrepresent the program or the team on the field, in the classroom, and in the community. In the movie *Remember the Titans*, Gerry Bertier asks the coach to cut his own friend from the team. "I know that Ray missed that block on purpose," Gerry says. "Sometimes you just got to cut a man loose." Ray's bad attitude and his refusal to play his position will hurt the team, on the field and in the community, and Bertier wouldn't allow his friend that level of negative influence.

Uncommon integrity is a difficult path to walk, but it is an inspiring and powerful way to live. An uncommon athlete chooses to maintain integrity every day—at practice, in competition, and in life.

1. Integrity is always a mark of true leadership. Do you agree or disagree? Why?

2. How can your team develop more integrity, on and off the field?

BE UNCOMMON

Integrity requires whole-hearted living. Everything you do, for your entire life, works together to build your reputation on and off the field. But one mistake can undo that reputation in a heartbeat. It is up to you to protect your integrity, making choices that build value into your name so that you can create a positive and powerful influence on those around you. No game, no hobby, no boyfriend or girlfriend, no Friday night "fun" is worth permanently damaging your name. Make integrity your goal.

OVERCOMING

UNCOMMON OVERCOMING

And they overcame him by the blood of the Lamb and by the word of their testimony, and they did not love their lives to the death. Revelation 12:11 (KJV)

Tamika Catchings has had an amazing career. She's played fifteen years in the WNBA, all of them with the Indiana Fever. She has won three Olympic gold medals and was named to the 2016 Olympic team that will compete in Rio. Heading into the 2016 season, she is the WNBA's active leader in points, rebounds, steals, and free throws. But Catchings is more than an impressive basketball player. She is also an uncommon overcomer.

Tamika Catchings was born with a hearing disability that affected both ears. As a child, she was teased over her hearing aids and speech impediment, and she struggled with being different.

But when she began to play basketball, everything changed. Sports gave Catchings an opportunity to define herself by how hard she worked, instead of by her disability. Despite her hearing impairment, she has excelled in sports and in life ever since, turning every difficulty into another possibility to do something great.

Think about it: The next level of success never requires you to go under; superior achievement always forces you to overcome.

1. What obstacles have you had to overcome to play your sport?

2. Do you know of anyone who, like Tamika Catchings, has faced major obstacles? How did he or she overcome those obstacles?

Every uncommon athlete must learn to face and overcome obstacles. And the key to overcoming every challenge is attitude. Outlook will always determine outcome. Every time. Not because a positive attitude makes everything go your way, but because having the attitude of an overcomer helps you see ahead to the goal you want to reach and keep going toward it, no matter what blocks your way.

Gertrude Ederle displayed this attitude. In 1925, Ederle attempted to swim the English Channel. Swimming the Channel is extremely hard. It's a distance of 21 miles at its narrowest point, the water is freezing cold, and swimmers have to fight the tide and the jellyfish. Ederle was determined to become the first woman ever to make it across, but her coach insisted that she quit after almost nine hours in the water.

Undaunted, Ederle found a new coach, continued her training, and in August 1926, completed her Channel swim in 14 ½ hours, two hours faster than the previous record. Ederle refused to be undone by people, circumstances, or her own doubts. And because she had an unflinching outlook, she accomplished a feat that no woman (and few men) before her had done. That is what uncommon overcomers do.

No matter the sport or the person, every athlete will eventually face an obstacle that will seem to be more than he or she can handle. It's often called "hitting the wall." It's the leg cramp in the last miles of the marathon. The one pass pattern that never seems to go right. The opponent who always seems to have the better record. But whether that wall is literal or not, an uncommon athlete will fight to get over it, around it, or through it. With a determined attitude, they get moving, keep moving, and stay confident until they find a way to conquer that mountain.

Uncommon athletes channel their passion, refusing to give up until they fight their way through. And like Gertrude Ederle, they will eventually find a way to get to the other side.

WORKOUT

1. How does your attitude affect your ability to overcome?

2. What are some obstacles that you or your team must fight against?

3. Is being an overcomer really worth the fight to get over "the wall"? How do you know?

WRAPUP

Now to him who is able to do immeasurably more than all we ask or imagine, according to his power that is at work within us, to him be glory in the church and in Christ Jesus throughout all generations, for ever and ever! Amen. Ephesians 3:20-21

Uncommon athletes must learn to be overcomers in every area of life. The obstacles of life can include illness, family problems, personal crises, or school issues, but no matter what giants stand against us, attitude is still the key to overcoming them.

First, we have to view our problems correctly. If we believe they are insurmountable, we will never find a way around. But when we see them as challenging but bearable, we can find the strength to overcome.

Attitude is always dependent on our view of God. David knew Goliath wasn't an unbeatable enemy; he saw how much bigger God was. Israel marched around the walls of Jericho because they trusted that God was able to deliver the city into their hands. The woman who touched Jesus' robe knew He was able to heal her, so she risked everything to come to Him for help.

In the same way, when we see God as powerful and able to handle whatever problems we

WRAPUP

face, we will depend on Him to help us overcome in every area of life.

1. Look again at Ephesians 3:20-21. How do these verses describe God?

Knowing that an all-powerful God is on our side, we can overcome the challenges of life. From working to pass the hard class, asking your dream date to the prom, or figuring out how to pay for college, challenges will come, but with God's help, they can be overcome. An uncommon athlete knows that each obstacle is an opportunity to watch God do something great.

And trusting in God's power also lets us overcome the drama of daily life. Sometimes, we don't have one specific giant to defeat. Instead, we will have to deal with the everyday issues of life: tension at home, bullying at school, time management, not missing the bus. But by relying on God's power, we can face these issues one day at a time until suddenly we find that we have managed them, defeated them, worked through them. We have overcome.

2. Overcoming is something we have to do in all of life. In what specific areas, outside of athletics, do you need to develop an attitude of overcoming?

3. How can you help someone else become an overcomer?

BE UNCOMMON

We rarely get a "do over," but we always have the chance to overcome. Life doesn't come with a pause button, and we cannot DVR a game or an opportunity to save it for later. Our challenge is to live today while keeping our focus on the end goal. Overcoming means seeing the difficulties, but focusing on getting to the other side of them. Work hard to succeed, but instead of being consumed by that success, set your sights on getting to the finish line in every area of life. No matter what you face, you can make it to "the other side." You can overcome.

STUDY 7

NERVE

UNCOMMON NERVE

. . . for God gave us a spirit not of fear but of power and love and self-control. 2 Timothy 1:7 (ESV)

He was at the top of his game. He'd finished the best season of his career and won gold in the 2008 Olympics. But in January of 2009, Michael Redd, a guard for the Milwaukee Bucks, blew his left knee, tearing both his ACL and MCL. The injury ended his season, but after months in rehab, Redd returned to start for the Bucks the next fall. Then, almost exactly one year after his injury, he again tore both ligaments in the same leg, ending his season early for a second year in a row.

For many athletes, one major injury would end their career. Coming back a second time would be impossible. But Michael Redd had uncommon nerve. He was determined to play in the NBA again. And after 14 months in rehab, he returned to the Bucks in March 2011, completing the season without further injury. Michael Redd played the following year for the Phoenix Suns before retiring from the NBA in 2013. His determination had paid off. He retired a champion.

Think about it: Dissect the nerves of a champion, and you're sure to find courage, spirit, and truth, affirmed with a boldness of faith—how can they lose?

1. What does the word determination mean to you?

2. Can you think of a time when you or someone you know showed great determination?

3. Why are "courage, spirit and truth" the foundation of uncommon nerve? How do they help you develop determination?

Developing uncommon nerve is about seeing the world as full of opportunities, not roadblocks. Where others see hardship and an excuse to give up, an uncommon athlete seizes the chance to do something great in the face of great difficulty. This kind of nerve means that you believe completely that you will succeed. It is an unflinching determination to accomplish your goals.

In 2003, Bethany Hamilton lost her arm to a tiger shark attack. She was floating on her board, arm dangling in the water, when the shark suddenly charged, biting off a chunk of her board and severing her arm just below the shoulder. In a single moment, her hopes of becoming a professional surfer became seemingly impossible. But Bethany was determined to find a way back. Three weeks after her accident, she was back in the water, learning how to surf with only one arm. In early 2004, she entered and won her first major surfing competition, and she continues to surf professionally.

Instead of hanging up her board when the unthinkable happened, Bethany Hamilton refused to give up. That is how uncommon athletes think. No matter what their circumstances are, no matter where they came from, and no matter what they have experienced, uncommon athletes have a passion that drives them. Every competition, every season, every challenge is a new possibility, and they reach forward to grab those chances. The bigger the game, the brighter the lights, the stronger his or her willingness to fight to the end. Like Bethany Hamilton, they decide, from the very beginning, that they are going to make it, and they keep going, no matter what comes their way.

But uncommon nerve is more than a drive forward. It also means refusing to retreat. Uncommon athletes do not back down; they do not turn tail and run. Like a general who burns the bridges behind his troops to cut off any retreat, an uncommon athlete will not turn back. When they get on the bus, when they arrive at the competition, there is no turning back until the mission is accomplished. As long as there is time on the clock, this athlete competes to win. They never give up. This is uncommon nerve.

WORKOUT

1. Why is determination so important in sports? What does it look like when an athlete lacks determination?

2. What habits can you start building right now to strengthen your determination?

3. Have you ever been tempted to give up or retreat? What kept you from doing it?

WRAPUP

Determination will always be a key ingredient to success, on the field and in life. Uncommon nerve means facing every challenge and refusing to give up.

Paul had this kind of determination. He traveled from city to city, telling people about Jesus. In some cities, he was welcomed. In many others, he faced arrest, beatings, and threats on his life. But no matter what happened, Paul kept preaching the truth about Jesus.

And Paul understood that, like us, his individual resources were not enough to handle the challenges he faced. Like us, he grew tired. He got discouraged. He ran out of energy and patience and strength.

But Paul also knew that God never does. And that's why God asks us to rely on Him instead of just ourselves. Uncommon nerve means drawing on God's resources to do what He has called us to do. Near the end of his life, Paul reminded his student Timothy that God "gave us a spirit not of fear, but of power and love and self-control" (2 Timothy 1:7). Timothy was a young man who faced great challenges as he continued the work Paul had started.. He had a lot to be afraid of, but Paul reminded him to depend on God

WRAPUP

and keep moving forward.

1. What does it look like to live in fear? What does it look like to live in "power and love and self-control?"

The Spirit of God will not lead us into fear, and He does not want us to make decisions out of fear. Instead, the Spirit floods us with power, with love, with the ability to live a controlled life. He enables us to live the life God designed for us, and nothing we fear will be able to defeat us. That is the source of uncommon nerve. When we live from His foundation—from power and love and self-control—we can fight with determination through the circumstances of life. God Himself is for us, and what He provides cannot be used up. He will always have more than enough power, more than enough grace, more than enough of whatever we need.

2. Read Philippians 4:17. What does God provide for us?

When we fall back on God's resources, He gives us an inner strength through His Spirit. Because God provides everything we need we can keep going towards all that He has called us to be and never back down. That's why we can be determined. That's why we can have uncommon nerve.

3. How does depending on the Spirit of God help you to live out the purpose God has called you to?

BE UNCOMMON

You will have many opportunities to walk away when things get hard. But uncommon nerve will help you see your fight through to the end. Whether it is a big game, a hard class, a tough decision, or a family crisis, you can succeed. Michael Jordan was passed over for varsity. Oprah Winfrey was once fired as a television reporter. Thomas Edison's teachers called him a failure. Each one of them eventually succeeded. They refused to let anything keep them from their dreams. They fought back and fought through, and they became great. You can live that uncommon nerve, too.

STUDY 8

PERSPECTIVE

UNCOMMON PERSPECTIVE

Do not be deceived: God cannot be mocked. A man reaps what he sows. Whoever sows to please their flesh, from the flesh will reap destruction; whoever sows to please the Spirit, from the Spirit will reap eternal life. Galatians 6:7-8

Every summer, the NFL holds its Rookie Symposium. It's a required, four-day training session where former players and staff address the realities and pitfalls of a professional football career. Former stars like Cris Carter and Warren Sapp talk about what helped them achieve great things. Others talk about the mistakes that ruined everything. They cover addictions, money, relationships, physical stress, and the hard reality that 40 percent of each rookie class will not be playing in three years.

Finally, players like Eddie George and Aeneas Williams encourage the rookies to consider, even before their first training camp, what they want their life to look like at the end. You want to wear the Hall of Fame jacket? You want to be a success when your playing days are over? Then live every day with uncommon perspective. See the end you want, and live today to make that end happen. That is the challenge given to the NFL rookies. And it is the challenge of the uncommon life as well.

Think about it: The person you will one day become is always a direct result of the choices you are making right now.

1. What does the phrase "Begin with the end in mind" mean to you?

2. Why would the NFL spend so much time talking about this principle with rookie players?

An uncommon athlete focuses on the long term. He or she knows that today not only defines the future, it decides it. Uncommon perspective sees that every today builds toward tomorrow. Going to practice today prepares you to compete later. Competing well on the reserve team now prepares you for varsity games later. Every step you take today will help you make the next step until you achieve great success.

However, uncommon perspective is uncommon. Out of the thousands who have played in the NFL, only 303 have made it to the Hall of Fame. Major League Baseball has enshrined only 310 players total, and the NBA and NHL have honored only 345 players and 268 players. These Hall of Famers are remembered because they pursued their sports well, playing each game with commitment and purpose, and created a legacy for themselves by their achievements. They lived with uncommon perspective.

But many more athletes choose the common road. The sports world is littered with the ruined careers and lives of men and women who lost their perspective and, as a result, lost everything else.

Ryan Leaf is one such athlete. Drafted second to Petyon Manning in 1998, he was expected to be great, but his attitude and behavior cost him everything. He skipped meetings, let his fame control him, and behaved poorly toward teammates, coaches, fans, and the media. To top it off, his on-field performance was mediocre. He was out of the NFL in four years and has spent the years since his retirement in and out of jail because of drugs.

Uncommon perspective could have saved Ryan Leaf. Had he chosen to live with PASSION, he might be looking back at a successful NFL career instead of fifteen years of chaos and decline. And Leaf is not alone. Dwight Gooden, Mike Tyson, and many others provide powerful examples of a life lived without uncommon perspective. An uncommon athlete will take those lessons to heart and choose the better way. He will live with perspective—keeping his eye on the destination even while standing at the starting line.

WORKOUT

1. What athletes can you name who have fallen because of a lack of perspective?

2. How does what you do today impact your future?

3. What short-term decisions can you make, right now, that will set you up for long-term success?

WRAPUP

Uncommon perspective is about delayed gratification. It is the self-discipline to put off getting something you want right now to get something better in the future. The best athletes in the world go to the gym every day so that, someday later, they will be able to keep going when it counts. They know eating healthy will enable them to perform at their best when the game is played. They know lifting weights is the harder, but surer, path to be ready for competition. They are willing to ignore the lesser temptations to achieve the biggest rewards in the end.

1. What are some "lesser gains" that might tempt you to give up on the long-term perspective?

2. Read Matthew 6:19-21. What does "lay up treasure" mean in these verses? What was Jesus trying to teach us about perspective?

Over and over, the Bible tells of men and women who gave up something now to gain something better in the end. Noah spent 100 years building a boat, even though he had never seen it rain. Moses left his home in Egypt's palace to live with the Jewish slaves. David refused to kill King Saul and waited almost twenty years to be

WRAPUP

made king. But God did not just give us good examples of perspective. He also gave us a specific warning about developing a long-term view of life.

3. Read Galatians 6:7-8. How would you explain the principle of sowing and reaping to someone else?

4. What does it means to sow "to please the flesh" and "to please the Spirit" in verse 8?

Sowing and reaping is a powerful illustration of uncommon perspective. Instead of demanding instant results, like microwave popcorn, the uncommon athlete trains himself to think like a farmer. Every farmer knows that what you put into the soil determines what you get out of it. He plants, he waters, he weeds, he waits, and finally, at the end, he harvests. Every farmer understands three principles:

1. You reap only what you sow.
2. You always reap later than you sow.
3. You always reap more than you sow.

5. How can you apply these principles of farming in sports and in life?

Like a farmer preparing his fields, the uncommon athlete understands that success comes with the long-term view. Instead of demanding everything now, uncommon perspective looks ahead and chooses wisely today to ensure great victory at the end.

BE UNCOMMON

Uncommon perspective is vital for success in sports and in life, but education is one of the most important areas to apply this view. Most people will succeed or fail based on their education. While there are exceptions, a person who barely passes or drops out of high school will face a difficult future. As hard as it is to be diligent in school, an uncommon athlete focuses on scholarship and athletics. Don't focus on the weight room to the exclusion of your homework. Make both a priority so you can set yourself up for a lifetime of success, on and off the field.

STUDY 9

USEFULNESS

UNCOMMON USEFULNESS

But in your hearts revere Christ as Lord. Always be prepared to give an answer to everyone who asks you to give the reason for the hope that you have. 1 Peter 3:15

Emmitt Smith is one of the greatest football players who ever competed. He is the NFL's all-time rushing leader. He had eleven straight 1,000-yard rushing seasons and helped propel the Dallas Cowboys into three Super Bowls in four years. He was elected to the Hall of Fame in 2010.

Emmitt Smith's success was built on an unbending commitment to consistency. In his Hall of Fame induction speech, Smith said, "Another critical principle is consistency. Consistency shows value. Consistency is necessary for trust, durability and longevity. You have to show up every week no matter how difficult the game or life might be. Over time consistency will allow you to achieve your goals."

Uncommon athletes are consistent. They are always ready, at a moment's notice, to do what needs to be done. And because they are consistent, they have uncommon usefulness—for the coach, for the team, for the community, and for themselves.

Think about it: Consistency shows value. Emmitt Smith said, "Consistency is necessary for trust, durability and longevity."

1. Do you agree with Emmitt Smith's quote? How did consistency help him succeed?

2. Do you consider yourself to be a consistent person?

Uncommon athletes understand that their highest goal, even more than winning, is to be useful; they want to be ready whenever the team needs them. And the foundation of uncommon usefulness is developing a habit of consistency.

An uncommon athlete is consistent in his time, his actions and his attitudes. He doesn't goof off, and his behavior is steady. He sticks to his routine and follows the rules, even when no one's looking. And he chooses not to overreact or lose his temper but responds respectfully every time.

As Emmitt Smith demonstrated in his fifteen-year football career, being consistent results in readiness. The uncommon athlete is able to jump into the game at a moment's notice. She can pick up the ball, come off the bench, or fill in for an injury. Because of her consistency, she is confident in her ability to perform, every time. She is ready.

But uncommon usefulness means others are confident in her abilities, too. The coach knows she has practiced faithfully and is ready to compete. Her teammates know they can rely on her, that she'll show up and compete well. That kind of uncommon athlete becomes a powerful tool for the team, a secret weapon already in place and ready to be used as soon as the opportunity presents itself.

Michael Phelps is a great example of this. Phelps has won a record 22 Olympic medals (18 gold). He is one of the greatest swimmers to ever compete. And, according to his coach, the key to his success is consistency. As a teenager, Phelps trained every day for 6 years; that's more than 2,100 days straight! Whether he wanted to or not, he showed up to swim. And because of that consistency, Phelps was always prepared on race day. He was ready to win when it was time to compete.

But Phelps's consistency also gave him usefulness. He competes in relays as well as in individual races. And his consistency in practice meant his teammates could count on him to be at the top of his form at every competition. He could support the team's effort to win the race, not simply shine as a solo competitor. That is uncommon usefulness.

WORKOUT

1. Which is more valuable on a team: a talented star player or a consistent support player?

2. Why can't an athlete be ready without being consistent?

3. What can you (or your team) do to be more useful to the coach and each other?

WRAPUP

In sports, in school, and in life, consistency is the key to uncommon usefulness. It means showing up every day, making mistakes and coming back anyway. On the field, this means being on time and ready for practices and games. It means doing drills and learning plays, spending time outside of practice to do the little things well. In school, this means doing homework every night so you don't fall behind. And in life, it means being disciplined and careful with your time, money, and relationships so that you can accomplish great things.

1. In which of these areas do you struggle the most to be consistent? Sports? School? Life?

Being consistent is not easy. The Apostle Peter learned this lesson the hard way. Hours before Jesus went to the cross, Peter had boasted that he would never leave; he would stay with Jesus no matter what. Before the morning came, Peter had not only abandoned Jesus, he had denied him three times. When the moment of truth came, Peter wasn't ready.

2. Have you ever promised to do something, but didn't see it through? How could consistency have helped you keep that promise?

After the resurrection, Jesus took Peter aside. Three times, He asked Peter, "Do you love me?"

WRAPUP

Three times, Peter answered, "Yes, Lord!" And all three times, Jesus gave him the same instruction: "Feed my sheep" (John 21). Jesus was telling Peter that it's not what happens in the "big" moments that defines greatness. True greatness is built on doing the little things well, over and over again.

That's why, many years later, Peter instructs us to do the same: "Always be prepared to give an answer to everyone who asks you to give the reason for the hope that you have" (1 Peter 3:15). In other words, Peter says, you have to do the work ahead of time. Practice. Be consistent. "Always be prepared."

3. Are you as prepared to talk about God or spiritual things as you are about sports or video games or another topic? What can you do to "always be prepared" to talk about God?

But God does not only want to use us to speak for Him. He also wants us to act on His behalf. He wants us ready and willing to do good things wherever we are.

4. Read 2 Timothy 2:21. What does Paul tell us it means to be useful to God?

In the same way uncommon usefulness means the coach knows we are always ready to play, in spiritual things, usefulness means we are ready to serve God wherever He directs us. We can obey him, do His good works, and live the lives He has created us for. That is the uncommon road. That is uncommon usefulness.

BE UNCOMMON

Readiness only comes with consistent preparation. To be ready on game night, we can't just practice free throws once a week; we have to spend hours every day shooting from the line. To be ready on test day, we can't cram the night before; we have to spend time every day doing our homework and keeping the information fresh. To be ready when God gives us opportunities, we can't just go to church when we feel like it; we have to read the Bible daily and spend time in prayer. When we are consistent, we become useful. Then we will be uncommon.

Reputation

UNCOMMON REPUTATION

A good name is more desirable than great riches; to be esteemed is better than silver or gold.
Proverbs 22:1

David Robinson, nicknamed The "Admiral" during his time at the Naval Academy, was a standout center for the San Antonio Spurs. He was league MVP in 1995 and won two championships with the Spurs, in 1999 and 2003. During his entire 14-year career, Robinson was admired on the court for his formidable skills and off the court for his commitment to his team and his community, even winning the 2003 *Sports Illustrated* Sportsperson of the Year Award.

But while Robinson worked hard to be the best on the court and in life, he especially understood the value of a good reputation. "What I need to do is have a great positive attitude and a great work ethic. Those two things validate me. Yes, it's important that I have good numbers, and I'm well-respected as a player. But I think it's more important that I'm respected as a man."

Think about it: "Reputation builds influence. Influence doesn't just happen. People have to trust you. They have to respect you. People have to believe you are someone worth listening to." Tim Brown, *Boys Won't Be Boys*

1. Work in groups of two or three and come up with your own definition for "reputation."

2. How is your reputation like your own personal brand (like Nike or Under Armor)?

3. What kind of influence has David Robinson had because of his reputation?

More than just focusing on an athlete's on-field performance, an uncommon reputation describes who that athlete is in every aspect of his or her life. David Robinson is a great example of this. He has always understood the value of a good reputation, and he has always been careful to maintain the integrity of his name.

On the court, David Robinson was outstanding, regularly posting high stats in scoring, rebounding and blocked shots. He is still considered one of the great centers of all time, but he was not focused on making a name for himself. Robinson was a team player. He fully supported every organization he was a part of. For example, though the Spurs drafted him in 1987, he fulfilled his two-year commitment to the Navy before joining the team. And once he began to play for San Antonio, he played his entire career for the Spurs. He always put the team first. He said, "I think any player will tell you that individual accomplishments help your ego, but . . . it counts more that the team has played well." His commitment to the team was also shown when the Spurs drafted Tim Duncan in 1997. Robinson willingly gave up the spotlight, helping to mentor Duncan even as he continued to play his best, and together they led the Spurs to the NBA Championship in 1999 and 2003.

Robinson is an uncommon athlete, and his reputation off the court was even more important to him than his on-court accomplishments. He is known for being kind and attentive to players, fans and the media. He has contributed so powerfully to the community of San Antonio that the winner of the NBA Community Assist Award now receives the David Robinson plaque. He even created a non-profit organization to assist other celebrities with their individual charitable investments.

David Robinson's life and career are unsullied by bad press, bad decisions, or personal misconduct. He was elected to the Hall of Fame in 2005, and in his speech, he praised his sons and wife, thanked his family and the Spurs organization, and thanked the audience for coming to share that moment with him. His humility, grace, and consideration of others made him great, on and off the court. He is the perfect example of what it takes to develop an uncommon reputation.

WORKOUT

1. Read Proverbs 20:7. What does this verse tell us about a good reputation?

2. How does having an uncommon reputation benefit you in your sport or competition?

3. Do you and your team, have a good reputation? Why or why not? What can you do to make your reputation better?

WRAPUP

David Robinson has spent his entire life building the reputation for which he is known. Every day, he stayed committed to his team, his family, his faith, and his community. The result is a reputation that inspires others. Unfortunately, gaining a reputation like Robinson's is not easy. An uncommon reputation takes a lifetime to build, but can be demolished in only a moment.

Just ask Marion Jones. In the 2000 Olympics in Sydney, Australia, she won three gold and two bronze medals in track. She was considered one of the fastest women alive and earned over a million dollars for each race she ran. But accusations of drug use haunted her, and finally in 2007, she admitted she had been doping for almost all of her career. She was sentenced to prison for six months, publicly apologized, and was stripped of her Olympic medals. Her reputation was ruined.

1. Jones cheated to win races and lost her reputation. What other behaviors or choices have cost someone you know their reputation?

An uncommon reputation is incredibly fragile. So an uncommon athlete must protect that reputation, recognizing that it is the most valuable asset he or she has. More than superior stats and high-profile contracts, an

WRAPUP

uncommon athlete knows that "a good name is more desirable than great riches" (Proverbs 22:1).

2. Do you desire a "good name" more than riches or good stats? Why or why not?

Protecting a reputation is not always easy. Every day, you will make choices that will either add value to your reputation or take away from it.

Thankfully, two simple principles are all you need to protect your reputation: think and wait.

Before you make a choice. before you do anything, think about it. Ask yourself questions about the choice. Is it wise? Will doing this hurt you? Will it hurt someone else? What might happen as a result of this decision? Think about what you're doing. And then, wait before you act. If someone is pressuring you, telling you how urgent it is for you to decide, back away. Give it an hour. Give it a day. Give yourself time to get some perspective so you can make a wise decision and protect your Reputation.

3. Have you ever saved yourself from a bad decision by choosing to think and wait? What happened?

4. Why is a reputation so easily destroyed? Why does one bad decision ruin a reputation? How can that reality help motivate you to protect your reputation?

BE UNCOMMON

Your reputation is the only thing anyone will remember about you after you are gone. It is a lifetime investment. Make it your highest goal to be remembered well. It's fine to want your number retired. It's great to pursue sports at the next level. But if your reputation is ruined, none of what you accomplish will matter. In middle school, in high school, in college, do everything you can to be the kind of person that others want to be like. Like David Robinson, make having an uncommon reputation your highest priority.

PERMANENCE

UNCOMMON PERMANENCE

The world and its desires pass away, but whoever does the will of God lives forever. 1 John 2:17

Almost every young athlete can recite the records held by great players. Babe Ruth, Michael Jordan, and many other champions are remembered for their great achievements. Consider these amazing numbers:

• Wilt Chamberlain scored 100 points in a single game in 1962. (Kobe Bryant ranks next with 81 points in a single game.)

• Cal Ripken played 2,632 straight baseball games, from May 1982 to September 1998. (Lou Gehrig is next with 2,130 games.)

• Wayne Gretzky scored 2,857 goals in his 21-year career in the NHL. (The next highest scorer is Mark Messier with 1,887.)

• Richard Petty drove his stock car for 200 wins. (David Pearson retired second with 105 wins.)

These records now seem unbreakable, and yet no record is guaranteed. No matter what numbers a player puts up, it is always possible that someone will beat even an "unbreakable" record. That's why an uncommon athlete focuses on a different kind of permanence. Instead of building a legacy on the shaky ground of setting records or winning games or celebrity status, uncommon athletes aim for an uncommon permanence.

Think about it: If you want to be remembered forever, you can't depend on a temporary foundation.

1. What sports record would you most love to break?

2. Sports achievements are one way people try to be remembered. In what other ways do people try to achieve permanence? Are any of these areas truly permanent?

Clint Dempsey understands what uncommon permanence is all about. Dempsey is a designated player for the Seattle Sounders and captain of the US National Team. He was the MLS Rookie of the Year in 2004 and has been named US Soccer Male Athlete of the Year three times in his career. He's had over 100 international appearances, he's played in England and the US, and he is a leading scorer for the men's national team in World Cup play. But Dempsey is much more than a soccer player.

Dempsey began playing soccer as a child and excelled at the game. His family drove him six hours, round trip, three days a week to play with advanced teams. But when he was 12 years old, his older sister developed a brain aneurysm and died. Losing her was hard on Dempsey. He had gone to church with his grandmother, but after his sister died, his faith was deeply shaken and then began to grow. Even though he continued to excel, he soon realized that there was more to life than soccer.

Even now, as a highly ranked soccer player in the US and in international play, Dempsey knows soccer is not all there is. He said, "My faith in Christ is what gives me confidence for the future. I know that through both good times and bad, He is faithful and will watch over me." Though he plays soccer to the best of his ability, scoring goals and breaking records, Dempsey knows that no sport can give him lasting value.

The Apostle John assures us "the world and its desires pass away, but whoever does the will of God lives forever" (1 John 2:17). No sports career can last forever. The best athletes retire or get injured. Only the one who is sold out to God will find lasting peace, on and off the field. Clint Dempsey displays this kind of powerful faith: "I play to the best of my abilities and am thankful for the many opportunities and amazing success He has given me. Through it all, I want to do right, not make mistakes, and live a life that is pleasing to Him." That focus is the path to uncommon permanence.

WORKOUT

1. Come up with your own definition of permanence and share your definition with your team.

2. Why is it easier to seek our permanence in the "world and its desires"? What are some of those desires?

3. What does "whoever does the will of God lives forever" mean? What would that look like for you?

WRAPUP

So we fix our eyes not on what is seen, but on what is unseen, since what is seen is temporary, but what is unseen is eternal (2 Corinthians 4:18). No award or record can give an athlete lasting permanence it's the same in life. Many people depend on the money in their bank accounts, their GPA, or today's clean bill of health to guarantee that nothing will ever hurt them. But outside circumstances cannot give uncommon permanence.

1. What does it mean to "fix our eyes on what is unseen"? What kind of things would Paul consider "unseen"?

Our lives are short, and an uncommon athlete understands there is more to life than what we can see or hold with our hands. While we cannot live forever, we can anchor our lives into a foundation that will give us uncommon permanence.

2. Read Psalm 90 as a team. Count the times this psalm talks about our years or our life.

Moses wrote Psalm 90. Moses was the leader of God's people, Israel when God freed them from slavery in Egypt. God used him to do some pretty big things like split the Red Sea, bring water out of a rock, and bring down the Ten Commandments. Moses was kind of a big deal, but even he longed to know that his life would have lasting meaning. He wanted to know his years were

WRAPUP

not wasted, and he wanted to find a hope that would continue even past death. That's why, in this psalm, Moses asks God to "teach us to number our days, that we may gain a heart of wisdom" (Psalm 90:12).

3. How can we learn to "number our days" and how can doing that lead us to wisdom?

Most people think that having permanence is about living a happy life and accomplishing great things. They think that, as long as things are going their way and they feel as if they're making a difference, they are basically okay. But Moses didn't see it that way. He knew that "being happy" wasn't always how life goes. And even though God used him to do amazing things, Moses knew that nothing he could do on his own would last.

4. Read Psalm 90:14. What does this verse tell us about how to have a happy life?

5. Read Psalm 90:17. Why can't our lives have uncommon permanence apart from God?

Moses understood the secret to uncommon permanence. To be uncommon, we have to ground our lives on something that will last forever, and only God can be that foundation. We need to understand that our lives are short, and we only have so much time to make a difference in our world. Because of this truth, we have to be intentional about how we live. We have to focus on making God our foundation in every area: in sports, in school, and in life. Only then will we find uncommon permanence.

BE UNCOMMON

It's hard to admit sometimes just how short each person's life really is. But every person on earth has been given a limited number of hours and years. An uncommon athlete knows this and relies on God to give him a firm foundation for his life. Making good grades, getting the scholarship, playing professional sports, or winning the championship are all wonderful goals. But they will not make anyone last forever. To have uncommon permanence, we have to live our lives—on and off the field—with God as our only foundation. That is the uncommon path.

OBJECTIVE

UNCOMMON OBJECTIVE

Looking forward . . . I press on toward the goal to win the prize for which God has called me heavenward in Christ Jesus. Philippians 3:13-14

In 2007, Tim Tebow was the first sophomore ever to win the Heisman Trophy, which recognizes the most outstanding college football player each year. But despite winning such a high honor, no trophy has ever been Tebow's primary goal. Instead, he has an uncommon objective.

While pregnant with Tim, his mother was very sick. They were living overseas, and her doctor recommended an abortion. His parents refused, trusting that God would save both mother and son. Tim Tebow was a miracle child, healthy in every way, and his parents encouraged him to use the life God had granted him to serve others and tell his story.

Which is exactly what Tebow has done. Even as he won awards, set records, and played in the NFL, Tim Tebow made God's glory his highest objective. The summer after winning the Heisman, Tebow said, "To be . . . someone that a parent can say to their kid, I want you to be like them. That's always been my dream and my goal more so than winning a trophy or winning a championship."

Think about it: Keep your eyes on your objective—your ultimate goal—and you'll be sure-footed in even the worst of circumstances.

1. What is your team's highest objective this season?

2. What would it look like to keep your focus on that objective at practice and in games?

The Heisman Trophy, the Stanley Cup, Olympic Gold, a World Cup trophy. These are the prizes for which athletes train all their lives. They give their time and energy with a single-minded focus to win their sport's highest prize. For many athletes, nothing is as important as the win. But an uncommon athlete knows winning the prize is not always the highest honor you can achieve.

In 2006, Canadian Sara Renner competed as a cross-country skier in the Turin Olympics. Just a few minutes into her final race, a competitor stepped on her pole, and it broke. Floundering, she watched as other sprinters began to pass her, but she could not keep up. Suddenly, someone handed her a pole. It wasn't perfect, but it was enough, and she resumed her race, finishing second to win an Olympic silver medal.

But this victory is not just about Sara Renner. It is also about someone who understands what it means to have an uncommon objective. Because the person who handed Renner the pole, keeping her in the race, was the Norwegian coach, Bjørnar Håkensmoen. It was his final Olympics as Norway's cross-country coach, and because he came to Renner's aid, the Norwegian team finished fourth, just missing a medal. Still, the coach was glad he did what he did. "How can you be proud of a medal you win when someone else's equipment is not working?" he asked.

Håkensmoen understood that our final objective cannot be limited to just a trophy, even an Olympic medal. For an uncommon athlete, a single award, even the championship itself, can never be the primary goal. Yes, he will train and push himself to perform well. Yes, she will compete to win the prize. But eventually, injury, retirement, or burnout will force every athlete to stop. And even winning "the big one" will last for only a moment. So an uncommon athlete understands true greatness comes from pursuing more than just a win. She knows sportsmanship, integrity, and fair play are just as important as the actual trophy. She pursues an uncommon objective, and it's a prize that can never be taken away.

WORKOUT

1. What was the uncommon objective on which Coach Håkensmoen focused?

2. Have you ever won a big game or an award? How did you feel at that moment? How did you feel a week later?

3. Why can't a medal or trophy or championship be our final Objective?

WRAPUP

Sam Snead was a golfer whose professional career spanned four decades. He won seven Majors, still holds the record for total PGA wins (82), and was inducted into the World Golf Hall of Fame in 1974. He died in 2002. But in 2013, the Snead family auctioned off a number of his trophies, medals, and golf clubs, giving most of the proceeds to charity. Snead's son commented, "The trophies didn't mean that much to Pop." Sam Snead was a world-class golfer who understood that the medals and trophies did not make him great. He was proud of his accomplishments, but he understood that life was about more than winning.

1. Do you like to keep and display your trophies? Why or why not? What do they represent to you?

Like Sam Snead, the Apostle Paul understood that nothing of lasting value can be found on earth. And Paul would know. In Philippians, chapter 3, he shares a long list of all of his religious accomplishments. In earthly terms, Paul was an MVP of the Jews. He was the best of the best. He'd had the best teachers, done the most work, proven himself better than anyone else. As far as Paul could tell, he was the champion.

And then Paul met Jesus. His religious zeal had inspired him to persecute Christians, and he was

WRAPUP

on his way to arrest even more believers. But Jesus stopped him, questioned him, and left him blinded for three days. And in the course of those days, Jesus changed Paul completely.

Once he met Jesus, Paul got a different perspective, a whole new way of seeing things. And suddenly, when compared with Jesus, all of his accomplishments meant nothing. "I consider them garbage," Paul said, "that I may gain Christ" (Phil. 3:8). Up until that moment, Paul's objective had been to make a name for himself, to be the most important person around. But once he met Jesus, Paul gained an uncommon objective—Jesus!

2. Why would Paul call his accomplishments "garbage"?

3. Have you ever realized the goal you were pursuing (maybe a trophy, a girl or guy, a GPA, a job) wasn't the best one to pursue? What did you do?

Like Paul, Tim Tebow knows his fame is a platform that God has given him to serve others. He reaches out to the less fortunate and loves to give back to the community. He knows that the best the world has to offer, including money, trophies, and an NFL career, is nothing compared to knowing Christ and living for him. That is better than a trophy. That is an uncommon objective.

4. Read Colossians 3:1-4. What do these verses teach us about what our objective should be?

BE UNCOMMON

Spend some time thinking about what your ultimate objective is right now. Is it straight-As? A winning season? A college scholarship? What are you spending your time, money, and energy pursuing? Write down what your objective is. Then ask yourself whether or not you are pursuing an uncommon objective. If it is not uncommon, what do you need to change or do to start working toward a lasting objective? Write down those new goals so you can begin to keep your eyes on an uncommon prize.

STUDY 13

Success

Uncommon Success

For what does it profit a man to gain the whole world and forfeit his soul? Mark 8:36 (ESV)

The Ryder Cup is a challenge tournament with US golfers playing against European players. Winners of each match earn one point, and the team with the most points wins the Cup.

In 1969, Jack Nicklaus was twenty-nine years old and playing in his first Ryder Cup. On the final day, the two teams were tied when the final pair, Nicklaus and Jacklin, began to play. The entire match rested on the last two golfers, and they were so evenly matched, the decision eventually came down to the 18th and final hole.

With his ball five feet from the hole, Jack Nicklaus could ensure at least a tie by sinking his final putt. He did it. The British golfer, Tony Jacklin, now had his chance. If he made his putt, the teams would tie. If he missed, the Americans would win. But before he could take his swing, Nicklaus reached down and picked up Jacklin's ball marker, conceding the shot to Jacklin. Instead of giving Jacklin the chance to miss, Nicklaus gave him credit for the putt, ending the match and the Ryder Cup in a tie.

Nicklaus knew the final score was not the main point. That is an uncommon attitude. That is uncommon Success.

Think about it: True success is about more than the final score; it's about the heart, soul, and behavior of those who have played the game.

1. The 1969 Ryder Cup was a tie. But who really won that day?

2. Name the most successful athlete you can think of. What makes him or her a success?

Uncommon success can never come through a win-at-all-costs attitude. No amount of cheating, no shortcut, and no final score will ever justify a win that isn't fair. In *The Karate Kid*, we see this principle in play. Daniel LaRusso must compete against a coach who demands that his students win, every time, no matter what. They cheat, injuring Daniel in the semi-final round and attacking his injury in the finals. But Daniel finally wins, proving that uncommon success means playing well and fighting fair, no matter what.

Many athletes today buy into the idea that the money they make or the records they set will define them as a champion. They want to win at all costs and think nothing of lying or cheating or doping to stay in the "winners" column. But an uncommon athlete understands that true success is not measured by the win-loss record. Uncommon success is measured by an entirely different set of rules.

Consider Andy Roddick. Roddick blasted his way onto the world tennis stage in 2003 and was a top-ranked player for a decade. He was known for his power serves and his on-court antics, sometimes losing his temper and earning costly penalties. But in one particular match, Roddick displayed uncommon success.

In 2005, Roddick had triple match point against Fernando Verdasco. Verdasco missed his first serve, and his second serve appeared to have missed as well. But as the umpire started to award Roddick the match and Verdasco came to the net to congratulate him, Roddick pointed out that the ball had, in fact, been in. The line judge changed the call, and the match continued with Roddick eventually losing to Verdasco.

Winning is always the goal in athletic competition. No athlete intends to lose. Uncommon athletes practice hard, play hard and push themselves so that they can, hopefully, win. But uncommon success is knowing that winning unfairly is not a true win. Roddick understood this. A moment of honesty cost him the match. He could have easily let the call go. No one would have even known about the line judge's error. But Roddick chose to do the right thing. He lost the match, but he achieved uncommon success.

WORKOUT

1. Have you ever been tempted to make or ignore a call so you or your team could win? Did you tell the truth, even if it cost you a point (or a win)?

2. Why is it better to do the right thing and lose the game than to win at all costs?

WRAPUP

Uncommon athletes know the final score is not the only definition of success. They play hard. But they also know there is more to life than the end of the game. Kerri Strug has that perspective. In 1996, Strug, an Olympic gymnast, fell in her first attempt on the vault and injured her ankle, but the team needed a higher score, so she lined up for her second vault. In a moment that has gone down in Olympic history, Strug completed her second vault perfectly, even with a sprained ankle, to give the American team their first-ever all-around gold medal.

Twenty years later, Kerri Strug lives a strong and vibrant life, raising her children and making a difference for underprivileged kids. This heroic athlete who was the definition of Olympic success in 1996 understands that her one moment of Olympic glory is not the crowning achievement of her life. She is more than her sport, more than her accomplishment.

David lived this way, too. Though he had been chosen as the next king of Israel, he refused to take the throne by force. As King Saul hunted him, David would not attack him. Though he could have killed Saul on two different occasions, David knew there was more to life than being made king. He waited for God's timing instead of rushing ahead to the final goal.

This is the same uncommon success Jesus was teaching in Mark 8:36. He asked his disciples

WRAPUP

(and us) a simple question: What does it profit a man to gain the whole world, yet forfeit his soul? Jesus wants us to understand that our life is not defined by what we achieve or earn or enjoy. No championship trophy, no million-dollar contract, no extravagant lifestyle will lead to uncommon success.

1. How can a man "gain the whole world"?

2. What did Jesus mean by "forfeit his soul"?

Uncommon success means understanding that what we accomplish cannot define our success. We can focus on sports or school or scholarships or status, and achieve great things in those areas, but none of them, by themselves, can give us uncommon success. We must have greater meaning and greater purpose in our lives, and neither of those can be built on the score of Friday night's game.

3. Why is it so easy to define our success on our accomplishments?

Uncommon success means living uncommon lives, doing the right thing and living with respect toward our opponents, our families, our neighbors, and ourselves. When we remember our souls are the most valuable part, not our bodies or our stats or our trophies, we can live our lives and play the game, so that we achieve uncommon success.

4. What can you do to pursue uncommon success in your school, your home, or your community?

BE UNCOMMON

Uncommon success means pursuing success the uncommon way. Honesty and sportsmanship are two of the primary qualities that lead to uncommon success. When you play your game, be a truth-teller. Own up to your mistakes, even if it costs you. Never lie to your coach, the ump, or your team. Be a good sport. Honor your teammates and your opponents above your own achievements. Play respectfully and according to the rules. Be willing to empower others, even as you do your very best. Play fair, play honest, and play to achieve uncommon success.

STUDY 14

ENDURANCE

UNCOMMON ENDURANCE

I have fought the good fight, I have finished the race, I have kept the faith. 2 Timothy 4:7

Wilma Rudolph contracted polio at age four, leaving her with a twisted leg and foot. Doctors told her she would never walk again. Instead, she became the fastest woman in the world, winning three gold medals in the 1960 Olympic games—the first woman ever to manage that feat!

Wilma Rudolph had to wear leg braces and endure years of therapy before she was able to compete. Her hard work paid off, and she quickly became a champion, running in two Olympic Games. But her endurance was tested outside of her sport as well. Rudolph is an African-American and a civil rights pioneer. She faced discrimination and worked to overcome it. In fact, her homecoming parade and banquet following the 1960 Olympics, were the first fully integrated events in her hometown.

Wilma Rudolph understood uncommon endurance. She said, "Nobody goes undefeated all the time. If you can pick up after a crushing defeat and go on to win again, you are going to be a champion someday." She retired from racing in 1962 and passed away in 1994, but because she endured, Wilma Rudolph will always be remembered as an uncommon athlete.

Think about it: Endurance means going the distance, pacing yourself to reach the end while pushing yourself to do the best that you can.

1. What parts of your sport require endurance from you (or your team)?

2. What makes endurance so difficult?

Uncommon endurance is not just about the miles run or the consecutive games played. Uncommon athletes focus on finishing well. They aim for a high goal and compete with all their heart, so that when they look back at the end, they can say they did well. While they can be tempted to give up or fade out, uncommon athletes move forward until the final buzzer sounds. Losing doesn't stop them and winning doesn't distract them from the ultimate finish line. Uncommon endurance means they fight through every difficulty to win big, even if they don't come in first.

Team Hoyt is a powerful example of this uncommon attitude. Dick Hoyt and his son, Rick, are long-distance competitors who run races together. But they are a very unique team. Rick Hoyt was born with cerebral palsy. He is wheelchair-bound and uses a special computer to communicate, but when he was 15, he told his dad he wanted to participate in a charity race. So his dad pushed him in the race, and Team Hoyt was born. Rick told his dad, "When I'm running, it feels like I'm not handicapped."

Since that race in 1977, father and son have run over 1,000 marathons, distance races, and triathlons together. They've even completed 6 ironman competitions and the Boston Marathon thirty-two times. For most of their running career, they competed in up to 50 races each year (though now they've cut back to only 20-25). After thirty years of racing, they finally decided the 2014 Boston Marathon would be their last long-distance race together, though Rick continues to compete with a good friend as his partner. In every race, the Hoyts' goal was always to finish well, and they have.

Team Hoyt displays uncommon endurance. Not only do they compete in long-distance competitions themselves, they have faced and overcome uncountable obstacles along the way, from Rick's medical issues to not being allowed to run in races. But they kept lining up. They kept running. And because they did, they have inspired millions of people with their story and their willingness to endure and to triumph.

WORKOUT

1. Why is endurance so important for an athlete to develop?

2. Do you think being part of a team helped the Hoyts develop uncommon endurance? Why or why not?

3. In what specific ways can you work to develop more endurance in your sport or with your team?

WRAPUP

Uncommon athletes want to have an enduring legacy. They want to have a name that lives on after them. But many high-profile athletes, though they have immense potential, never fully develop into all they could be. Like Penny Hardaway, Duante Culpepper, and Monica Seles, many athletes have powerful beginnings. But they could not compete long-term, and their careers ended with only hints of the greatness they might have achieved.

Bo Jackson is a great example of an incomplete legacy. Jackson is the only player to be named an All-Star in both the NFL and MLB, but a hit from behind popped his hip out of place. He required a hip replacement surgery, ending his career in the NFL. He managed a comeback in baseball, but retired after competing for only one more season. Bo Jackson had so much potential, but his career ended before he could fully develop his legacy.

1. Which athletes do you think have an incomplete legacy? What kept them from enduring (injury, bad decisions, other problems)?

Uncommon athletes, on the other hand, leave a lasting mark on the game, their fans and even the world. Many of them have been mentioned already in this book. From Emmitt Smith, Jerry Rice, and David Robinson, these athletes have enduring legacies. They protected their names and endured long-term. And they

WRAPUP

continue to inspire others to work hard and serve as an example for future athletes. Endurance doesn't always equal fame though. For many coaches and athletes, an enduring legacy is made playing as an amateur or coaching high school teams or supporting the Special Olympics. Whether they are world-famous or not, uncommon athletes know their names will live on, for all the right reasons.

2. What athletes (famous or not) can you name who have left an uncommon legacy? What can you learn from their success?

Uncommon endurance was the Apostle Paul's perspective, too. As he looked back over his life, he could say to Timothy, "I have fought the good fight, I have finished the race, I have kept the faith." Though he was imprisoned in a Roman jail, facing execution, Paul knew that he had finished well. In every area that mattered —in life, in ministry, in relationships—Paul knew the legacy he left behind would endure. Like Paul, we can develop uncommon endurance and leave behind a lasting name.

3. What was the legacy Paul left for us to follow?

4. Why do you think Paul wrote these words to Timothy? To encourage him? To inspire him? If you were Timothy, what would your reaction be to Paul's final letter?

5. If your life ended suddenly, what kind of legacy would you leave? Would your life display uncommon endurance? If not, what can you change so you can finish well?

BE UNCOMMON

Finishing well is the proof of uncommon endurance, but finishing well is not easy. It takes a long-term perspective, a commitment to doing all of life well, and an ability to get up when losses happen. We need endurance in every area of life: in school, at our job, in our families, in our neighborhoods. Whether your finish line is high school graduation or the 100-yard dash, make a commitment today to develop uncommon endurance. Write out the goal. Date it. Sign your name, and put it where you can see it often. The road to finishing well starts today, and you can choose to be on it.